Leslie Miles

Spre

by

Robert Hahn

*Can layer the interpretation

CreateSpace

www.CreateSpace.com

Copyright © 2010 Robert Hahn

All rights reserved. No part of this book may be reproduced in any format without the written permission of the author, except in the case of brief quotations in critical articles and reviews.

Ator Tarot card images © 2001 and used by permission of

Glow In The Dark, llc.

www.glowinthedarkpictures.com

First Edition

Printed in the United States of America

Acknowledgements

A book is not written in a vacuum; it is in many ways a collaborative effort. Such is the case with this book, and I offer heartfelt thanks to the following individuals:

Margaret Letzkus, who created the cover and worked on the editing and formatting – your friendship, love and support over the years have meant more than I can possibly say.

Robin Ator, creator of the delightful Ator Tarot – many thanks for permission to use your wonderfully whimsical deck to illustrate the book.

Joanna Powell Colbert and Teressena Bakens, gifted and respected Tarot artists and teachers -- your support of the book has inspired me and affirmed that my work may inspire others. Thank you for being part of my Tarot Tribe!

The members of our local Tarot Circle – you were all my beloved guinea pigs as I was creating these spreads, and you enthusiastically took them to heart. Thank you so much!

Phillip Guillory, my wonderful partner and technology guru – without you, this book would have never seen the light of day!

Table of Contents

Introduction	vi
The Fool Spread	2
The Magician Spread	4
The High Priestess Spread	6
The Empress Spread	8
The Emperor Spread	10
The Hierophant Spread	12
The Lovers Spread	14
The Chariot Spread	16
Strength Spread	18
The Hermit Spread	20
Wheel of Fortune Spread	22
Justice Spread	24
The Hanged Man Spread	26
Death Spread	28
Temperance Spread	30
The Devil Spread	32
The Tower Spread	34
The Star Spread	36
The Moon Spread	38
The Sun Spread	40
Judgement Spread	42
The World Spread	44
Bibliography	46

Introduction

The mysterious and beautiful images of the Tarot have fascinated people for hundreds of years. Whether used for gaming, fortune telling, ceremonial magic or self-exploration, these images continue to haunt our imagination.

There are hundreds of spreads available to use with the Tarot, so why another collection? As a teacher of the Tarot, I was looking for novel ways to help students understand the symbolism and meanings of the cards. The Major Arcana of the Rider Waite Smith (RWS) deck is full of esoteric symbolism used to depict meaning. I came up with the idea of creating spreads for each of the Majors, using some of the cards' symbolism as inspiration for the spread positions. The Ator Tarot, used in this book, retains most of the RWS symbolism.

The members of the Tarot Circle, which I co-facilitate, were the guinea pigs for these spreads. Over a period of several months, they looked forward to them and asked when the next one would be introduced. The spreads were popular and seemed to help the group remember aspects of the meanings of the cards.

How to Use This Book

This book can be used by both beginners and experienced readers. It is often hard to come up with questions to read about, so these spreads offer an interesting alternative. Although the spreads are based on each of the Major Arcana, the spreads can offer enlightening wisdom and advice.

Teachers may use this book in conjunction with their Tarot classes. They may find, as I did, that the spreads help students understand the symbolism and more easily remember the meanings.

The spreads are very flexible as well. Teachers who have different meanings for the symbols can substitute their own preferences. Symbols are very fluid and can have a range of meanings. Individuals using the book can also substitute their preferred meanings for symbols in the spreads. Included in the bibliography are some books on symbolism (both general and Tarot-specific) that I have found useful.

Readers who use decks other than the RWS may adapt the spreads to their own decks and the symbols they incorporate. The questions may also be changed or adapted to suit individual needs and preferences.

Readers wishing to incorporate astrology will find a table of correspondences at the back of the book.

In addition, the spreads can be used more than once. As our personal circumstances change, the spreads may offer new insights on both the spiritual and mundane aspects of our lives. Feel free to experiment with the spreads, find your own ways of using them, and perhaps, even create spreads for the Minor Arcana. Above all, have fun and enjoy your study of the Tarot!

Themes for the Fool:

Innocence, spontaneity, freedom, impulsivity, leap of faith, adventure, potential, innovation

Naïve, non-serious, distracted, silly, foolish, careless

The Fool Spread

1. The sun – What is your inspiration? What sparks your journey?

2. The bag – What do you need for your journey?

3. The mountains - What knowledge do you bring with you for your journey?

4. The white rose – How do you feel about your journey?

5. The dog – Who, or what, tries to hold you back?

6. The cliff's edge – Your first step: where might it take you?

7. What is the Fool's message for you?

Themes for the Magician:

Manifestation, creation, will, intent, confidence, action, channeling divine will

Inflated ego, misuse of talents, trickery

Handwritten notes:
- Intent
- consciousness
- Balance
- Connection to Spirit
- manipulation
- egotism
- undisciplined

The Magician Spread

1. The wand in the hand – What Divine energy are you connected to?

2. The lowered hand – How or where do you welcome Divine energy into your life?

3. The pentacle – What do you value most about your ability to manifest what you desire?

4. The cup – How do you feel about manifesting what you desire?

5. The sword – How can you effectively visualize what you seek to manifest?

6. The wand – What inspires you to manifest what you desire?

7. What is the Magician's message for you?

Handwritten notes:
- 7. Red + wh. flowers – How can you use clarity + passion to fuel manifestation
- 8. reminiscate – How do you stay connected – clarity
- red flowers – clarity
- white flows passion

Handwritten annotations around the card:
- duality
- inner knowledge
- spiritual-mental aspects of the Divine Feminine
- being not doing
- subconscious revelation

Themes for the High Priestess:

Inner wisdom, mystery, intuition, feminine power, reflection, hidden knowledge

Secrecy, aloofness, ignoring guidance from spirit

The High Priestess Spread

1. The Isis crown (symbol of the Divine Feminine) – How or where can you best use your intuition?

2. The black Pillar of Severity on the Tree of Life – Where in your life are you rigid, inflexible, or subjective?

3. The white Pillar of Mercy on the Tree of Life – Where in your life are you flexible or objective?

4. The Priestess (middle pillar) – Where or how do you synthesize or find balance between cards 2 and 3?

5. The Torah – What is your inner Truth?

6. The crescent moon – How can you balance your intuition and emotions?

7. Behind the veil of pomegranates – What is the High Priestess' message for you?

What separates you from your source of infinite wisdom

8 – What is the HP msg for you

Themes for the Empress:

Abundance, fertility, pleasure, comfort, creativity, pregnancy (literal or figurative), maternal energy

Overindulgence, greed, laziness, over-protective, smothering

The Empress Spread

1. The crown of 12 stars – What inspires your creativity?

2. The scepter – How can you best use your earthly power?

3. Venus (glyph on the heart) – How can you best express your loving nature?

4. The cushions – What gives you comfort?

5. The grain – What seeds do you need to plant in your life? What do you need to harvest in your life?

6. The waterfall – How can you best allow your abundance to flow?

7. What positive or comforting lesson(s) have you learned from your mother?

8. What is the Empress' message for you?

Themes for the Emperor:

Authority, control, limits, power, stability, leadership, paternal energy

Tyranny, authoritarian, abuse of power, unstable, aggression, lack of leadership

The Emperor Spread

1. The throne - How comfortable are you with your own authority or power?

2. The number four (iv) - Where do you need balance and stability?

3. Aries (ram heads on top corners and armrests of throne) - What do you seek to initiate or conquer?

4. The ankh scepter - Where do you need to focus your energy now?

5. The armor - Where are you potentially rigid or inflexible?

6. What positive or empowering lesson(s) have you learned from your father?

7. What is the Emperor's message for you?

Themes for the Hierophant:

Teaching, guidance, spiritual authority, wisdom, conformity, traditions, orthodoxy, blessings

Dogmatic, judgmental, intolerant, guilt, rigidity, abuse of rules

The Hierophant Spread

1. The Hierophant (spiritual teacher) – What do you have to teach others?

2. The columns – What supports you on your spiritual path?

3. The triple crown (symbol of authority) – What authority do people recognize in you?

4. Astrological correspondence with Taurus – How does your spirituality comfort you?

5. The hand raised in benediction – What blessings do you share with others?

6. Acolytes – What kind of wisdom do you seek from others?

7. Keys (lineage) – What formal or familial teachings or traditions are important in your life today?

8. What is the Hierophant's message for you?

Themes for the Lovers:

Love, romance, passion, relationships, communication, partnerships, attraction, choices

Jealousy, obsession, poor communication, lack of desirability or passion, poor choices

The Lovers Spread

1. The man (conscious self) – What do you consciously seek in a relationship?

2. The woman (unconscious self) – What do you unconsciously seek in a relationship?

3. The angel (higher consciousness) - What blessing or lesson might you learn from your relationship(s)?

4. Nudity of the couple – How you can be totally open and honest in your relationship(s)?

5. The snake – How can relationships change you?

6. The mountain – What are your goals for a successful relationship?

7. Astrological correspondence with Gemini – How can you successfully communicate in your relationship(s)?

8. What is the Lovers' message for you?

Themes for the Chariot:

Forward movement, victory, success, vehicles, mental control, choices of direction

Delays, stalled plans, lost success, resting on your laurels

The Chariot Spread

1. How is your vehicle (literally)?

2. How is your physical body (also a vehicle)?

3. How ready are you to move forward?

4. The black sphinx - In which direction(s) can you go?

5. The white sphinx - What other direction(s) are possible?

6. What could prevent you from moving forward?

7. What is the Chariot's message for you?

Themes for Strength:

Power, inner strength, vitality, self-esteem, holding your tongue, control of instincts or animal nature

Weakness, fear of speaking out, letting your instincts control you, lack of self-esteem

Strength Spread

1. The lion – How can you best use your physical strength?

2. The woman – How can you best use your inner strength?

3. What needs to be tamed in your life?

4. What do you need to express or not hold back?

5. How can you best follow your instincts?

6. The lemniscate – How can you best integrate your physical and inner strength?

7. What is Strength's message for you?

Themes for the Hermit:

Solitude, withdrawal, introspection, meditation, wisdom, seeking higher truths, guru or teacher, prudence

Hiding, loner, ignoring wisdom, lack of prudence

The Hermit Spread

1. The lantern – How are you letting your light shine?

2. The staff – Where could you use additional support?

3. The cloak (wisdom) – How can you make the most of what you have learned?

4. The mountain – What kind of higher wisdom are you seeking?

5. Looking to the left - What issues or lessons from the past may help illuminate your higher wisdom?

6. In older decks, the lantern was sometimes depicted as an hourglass – What do you need to complete before the sands run out?

7. What is the Hermit's message for you?

Themes for the Wheel of Fortune:

Change, fortune, cycles, destiny, luck, chance, what goes up must come down, taking risk(s)

Bad luck, loss of fortune, going against the flow, stubbornness

Wheel of Fortune Spread

1. What changes have begun to manifest in your life?

2. The Sphinx – What higher wisdom do you need during this time of change?

3. The red figure of Anubis – What do you need to do during this time of change?

4. The snake Typhon – What do you need to release during this time of change?

The four beings in the corners of the Wheel are (clockwise from top left):

5. Aquarius (air) – The effect of change on your ideas, thoughts, or communication.

6. Scorpio (water) – The emotional effect of change.

7. Leo (fire) – The effect of change on your energy or creativity.

8. Taurus (earth) – The practical lesson(s) you may learn from any changes in your life.

9. What is the Wheel of Fortune's message for you?

Themes for Justice:

Balance, fairness, discernment, karma, legal matters, contracts

Imbalance, injustice, abuse of power, judgemental, overly critical, bureaucracy

Justice Spread

1. Where do you need balance, fairness or a decision made in your life?

2. The sword – How discerning or rational are you about the issue raised in question 1?

3. No blindfold - How can you see all sides of the issue clearly and objectively?

4. The scales –Toward which option do your scales tip? Are you leaning toward a decision?

5. The red gown – How does your passion for fairness affect your decision(s)?

6. The pillars and the veil – What wisdom, knowledge, or experience do you use when making decisions?

7. Action – What can you do to bring balance or fairness into your life?

8. What is Justice's message for you?

Themes for The Hanged Man:

Seeing things from a new perspective, self-sacrifice, enlightenment, initiation, self-restraint

Where you are stuck, refusal to consider other perspectives, lack of enlightenment, lack of restraint

The Hanged Man Spread

1. Suspension - What are you "hung up" on? Where are you experiencing inertia in your life? What is on hold? Where do you feel stuck?

2. Sacrifice - What sacrifice(s) are you making in your life now?

3. Inversion - What new perspective(s) may help you see things clearly?

4. Initiation - What do you need to do differently in your life?

5. Nimbus (the halo) - What lesson(s) can you learn from this situation?

6. What is the Hanged Man's message for you?

Themes for Death:

Transition, change, transformation, letting go of what is no longer useful

Refusal to change, loss, failure, holding on to old habits or relationships

Death Spread

1. Death on horseback – When change or transformation enters your life, how might you respond?

2. The mystic rose – When you change or transform yourself, what might develop as a result?

3. The fallen king – What part of your ego, power or control might need to be changed or released?

4. The Hierophant – What part of your belief system might need to be changed or released?

5. The children – What ideas, teachings, or beliefs that you carry from childhood might need to be changed or released?

6. The rising sun – What new beginnings are dawning for you now?

7. What is Death's message for you?

Themes for Temperance:

Blending, synthesis, combination, moderation, control, testing the waters

Extremes, lack of moderation, lack of control

Temperance Spread

1. The angel – What spiritual guidance are you being offered?

2. The third eye - What do you instinctively know that needs to be tempered or moderated?

For cards 3 and 4, consider these questions using two cards:

> The cups – Which aspects of your life need to be carefully combined at this time? What might be the result?

5. The foot in the water – What new "waters" are you testing in your life?

6. The setting sun and path – What has brought you to this place; to this next step; to this test?

7. The irises – What message does Temperance have for you?

Themes for The Devil:

Seeing through illusions, renovation, comedy, silliness, light coming out of the darkness, creating

Bondage, shadow, materialism, obsession, delusion, temptation, impulsivity, abuse, addiction, excessiveness, violence, selfishness

The Devil Spread

1. Dark background (your blind spot) - In which area(s) of your life do you not see clearly? How would clarity help you?

2. The man in chains - What are you consciously bound to, addicted to, or chained by?

3. The woman in chains - What are you unconsciously bound to, addicted to, or chained by?

4. The inverted pentagram - In which area(s) of your life do you allow your desires, illusions, or fears to control you?

5. Devil's talons - What do you grasp onto, or have trouble letting go of?

6. The inverted torch – How is your energy or creativity misplaced in your life?

7. What is the Devil's message for you?

epiphany — changes your world — makes it all a kilter — can't go back

THE TOWER

Themes for The Tower:

Breakthrough, breaking out of rigid thinking and habits, sudden insights, "aha" moment, major cleansing

Destruction, upheaval, fall from grace, inflated ego

The Tower Spread

1. The tower – What has become so rigid in your life that it needs to be cleared away or destroyed?

2. The lightning bolt – What revelation do you need to be "struck by" in order for the cleansing or destruction to occur?

3. The crown – How can you stop trying to control major changes in your life?

4. The falling figures – How might you react to this experience? How might it affect you? Will you jump for your life, abandon ship, or go with the flow?

5. Yods – What divine grace is given to you during this experience to help you through?

6. The number of the Tower (16) reduces to (7) The Chariot – How can you move forward as a result of this experience?

7. What is the Tower's message for you?

Themes for The Star:

Hope, faith, optimism, wishes, healing, reflection, illumination, protection

Pessimism, hopelessness, disillusionment, anxiety, self-doubt

The Star Spread

1. The healing star – What healing or cleansing is needed in your life right now?

2. The naked woman – What do you need to do to facilitate this healing or cleansing?

3. The Scarlet Ibis (bird sacred to the Egyptian god Thoth) – What does your higher self tell you?

4. The pool – What does your subconscious tell you?

5. The pitcher of water poured on the land – What does your conscious mind tell you?

6. The Seven Stars – What message do the stars have for you?

7. How are you the star of your own life?

Themes for The Moon:

Psychic abilities, cycles, intuition, spiritual evolution

Illusion, not seeing clearly, mystery, deception, instincts, uncertainty, escapism, unclear thinking, vague or hidden fears, warnings

The Moon Spread

1. The crayfish - What message or issue from your unconscious is trying to become conscious?

2. The path - Where might this message or issue lead you?

3. The dog - How might you rationally respond to the issue?

4. The wolf - How might you instinctively respond to the issue?

5. The pillars - Through what kind of gate, experience, or transition must you pass in order to resolve the issue?

6. The mountains - What is the lesson, wisdom, or higher truth you may learn?

7. The Moon - How can your intuition guide you?

8. What is the Moon's message for you?

Themes for The Sun:

Happiness, innocence, freedom, energy, vitality, healthy ego, illumination

Burnout, excessive ego, pessimism, depression, delayed success

The Sun Spread

1. The Sun – How does your authentic self shine in the world?

2. The child – How can you allow your child-self to express joy, happiness, playfulness, and a sense of wonder?

3. The child's open arms – How can you openly embrace or welcome such expression(s)?

4. The red flag – What are you passionate about in your life right now? What inspires you?

5. The horse without reins – Where might your unconscious desires take you?

6. The sunflowers – What have you accomplished in your life?

7. The stone wall – What obstacles or boundaries have you overcome and left behind?

8. What is the Sun's message for you?

Themes for Judgement:

Rebirth, change, growth, renewal, answering the call, consciousness, new direction, break from convention

Judgemental, unwelcome change, lack of growth, separation, unwillingness to move on

Judgement Spread

1. The angel with the horn - What are you being called to do?

2. The cross - In which new direction(s) might the call take you?

3. The man praying - What have you been praying for or seeking?

4. The child with open arms - What do you need to embrace?

5. The woman with outstretched arms - What are you seeking to bring into your life?

6. The coffins - What has been holding you back from answering the call? What old habits or beliefs are restricting you?

7. Literally – How or where are you being too judgemental in your life?

8. What is Judgement's message for you?

Themes for The World:

Culmination, completion, integration, wholeness, having it all, fulfillment, threshold of a new beginning

Excess, lack of completion, unwillingness or fear of moving forward

The World Spread

1. The wreath - Where has your path lead you so far? Where might your next step lead you?

2. The dancing figure – How do you dance in celebration of the accomplishments of your life?

3. The wands - How or where have you integrated your spiritual and worldly power?

4. The bull (Taurus) - What values keep you grounded as you take the next step?

5. The lion (Leo) - How or where can you best use your energy as you move forward?

6. The eagle (Scorpio) - What do you need to see with eagle-eye clarity as you step into the unknown?

7. The man (Aquarius) - What support from your family or community will help you move forward?

8. What is the World's message for you?

Bibliography

There are many books available on Tarot and symbolism. Here are some of my favorites, which I found useful in the creation of this book.

Tarot Symbolism:

Amberstone, Wald and Ruth Ann. <u>The Secret Language of the Tarot</u>. San Francisco, CA: Red Wheel/Weiser, 2008.

Pollack, Rachel. <u>Rachel Pollack's Tarot Wisdom: Spiritual Teachings and Deeper Meanings</u>. Woodbury, MN: Llewellyn Worldwide, 2008.

Thompson, Sandra A. <u>Pictures from the Heart: A Tarot Dictionary</u>. New York, NY: St. Martin's Press, 2003.

General Symbolism:

<u>Signs and Symbols: An Illustrated Guide to Their Origins and Meanings</u>. New York, NY: DK Publishing, 2008.

O'Connell, Mark and R. Airey. <u>The Complete Encyclopedia of Signs and Symbols</u>. London: Hermes House, 2006.

Astrological Correspondences

The following are the astrological correspondences of the Hermetic Order of the Golden Dawn (GD). Those who use other correspondences may prefer to substitute alternative attributions. The Golden Dawn used only the seven classical planets. The inclusion of Uranus, Neptune, and Pluto are modern correspondences.

The Fool	Air (GD), Uranus
The Magician	Mercury
The High Priestess	Moon
The Empress	Venus
The Emperor	Aries
The Hierophant	Taurus
The Lovers	Gemini
The Chariot	Cancer
Strength	Leo
The Hermit	Virgo
The Wheel of Fortune	Jupiter
Justice	Libra
The Hanged Man	Water (GD), Neptune
Death	Scorpio
Temperance	Sagittarius
The Devil	Capricorn
The Tower	Mars
The Star	Aquarius
The Moon	Pisces
The Sun	Sun
Judgement	Fire (GD), Pluto
The World	Saturn

About the author

Robert Hahn, M.A., is a Tarot teacher and reader who lives in the desert Southwest. He has worked with the Tarot for more than 15 years, and has studied with renowned Tarot teachers Geraldine Ameral, Mary Greer, Rachel Pollack as well as Ruth Ann and Wald Amberstone. Robert's other studies include astrology, numerology, Qabalah, and Reiki. He is a member of Tarot Professionals and enjoys collecting Tarot and oracle decks. Robert can often be found attending the Bay Area Tarot Symposium (BATS) and the Tarot School's Readers Studio.

Robert can be found online at www.desertoracle.net.

Made in the USA
Coppell, TX
07 September 2020